Praying to the Black Cat

Henry Israeli

Praying to the Black Cat

Henry Israeli

—Del Sol Press　•　Washington, DC

Also by Henry Israeli:

New Messiahs

Translated and Edited by Henry Israeli:
Fresco: Selected Poetry of Luljeta Lleshanaku
Child of Nature

Del Sol Press, Washington, D.C.

Paper ISBN: 978-1-934832-10-3

First Edition

Cover Image: Dawn Black, *Venus of Willendorf Incarnate*, 22" x 30", gouache, watercolor, and ink on paper, 2009, Collection of James Alefantis

Publication by Del Sol Press/Web Del Sol Association, a not-for-profit corporation under section 501(c)(3) of the United States Internal Revenue Code.

Acknowledgements

The author would like to thank the following journals (and their editors) in which versions of many of these poems first appeared: *The Canary, Fence, The Konundrum Engine Literary Review, The Literary Review, Luna, Margie, Ninth Letter, Passages North, Per Contra, Pool, Rattapallax, Seneca Review, Spinning Jenny,* and *Tin House.*

Many thanks to Forrest Gander, Jane Miller, and Timothy Liu for their insight, advice, and encouragement.

Thanks to Michael Neff and the folks at Del Sol.

Who in the rainbow can draw the line where the violet tint
ends and the orange tint begins? Distinctly we see the
difference of the colors, but where exactly does the one first
blendingly enter into the other? So with sanity and insanity.

—Herman Melville, *Billy Budd*

Table of Contents

for Danielle

who lifted me up from the depths

IT BEATS AS IT WOULD FALL IN TWENTY PIECES

The instruments of my torture
laid out before me.

Who are they. Collectively, individually, from
                                    scene to scene

sporadic images flash behind
                              the screen.

Are you ready? No answer.
           Are you ready? The erotic forever

third-personing against
               the backdrop.

Door hinge unleashes   iambs into
      the lyric

afterburner. Someone asks a question
and suddenly five people surround her with

deciphering looks.
                         What language do you speak?

Words batter against a window.

Where are we?   No answer.

In case you haven't noticed.
It's a kind of humor.

                              At work here.

Feeling better?   No answer.

Laughter like the death throes
        of a typewriter. Small light

blinks on. Down we go. Blinks off.
                        The room

tighter now than skin.

Welcome to

            The Guest Room.

I

DEMENTIA

The shadow on the wall
        mocks movement. We lie
back to back, goldfish circle
        inside the wineglass
you lift to your lips. The blue walls,
        reverberate, fade out.
Our asses touch, yours
        smooth, mine reptilian,
the difference electricity:
        the air burns with it;
the night is crushed in it.
        "Your turn now," you say.
And the rain, the rain,
        soaking us through and through.

CREATION MYTH NUMBER ONE

In the House of Abandoned Children a boy leans over to watch a spider wrap a fly, a fragile gift. There is a tenderness here not unlike mothering, a caring in the way the handless arms turn the prey round and round, wrapping it in varying diagonal threads until it becomes a swaddled white ball. In hooked mandibles the spider holds the trophy up over her head. For the spider, the boy's face is a planet or god, a blessing. The boy, bored now, pinches the spider between thumb and forefinger—how its milky brain pops out! *Bad Mommy*, says the boy, unwrapping the fly from its silky casing. The fly vomits, then flits and buzzes about the boy's ears. Mad with disillusion and regret, the boy climbs to the roof and leaps. To his amazement he rises upward, the house shrinking beneath him. *Funny*, he thinks, *from here the House of Abandoned Children looks so, so....* He reaches down and crushes it with one little twist of his thumb, its light bursting out to fill the vastness of the night sky with stars.

CREATION MYTH NUMBER TWO

My parents were born old—shrunken, weathered, gnome-like. As children they crouched under fallen branches, hiding from dogs that sniff out ugliness and decay. They burrowed underground, but at last emerged, sunlight stinging their blood-tinged eyes. Holding hands while walking across dusty fields, they contemplated what life would have in store for two born as decrepit as they. Wept for themselves they did, and slept fitfully, liver spots on their gnarled hands, faint memory of stars long submerged. Hunched, feet cracked and fissured, they reached the city walls, begged entrance. No one paid them any mind. No one slipped them between and around the legs of giants. When their eldest daughter was born, they barely could remember having been *merely old*. When a second daughter arrived they were true ancients, bones carbon black, skin stacked in leather ringlets, facial features indistinguishable. Teeth? Gone. Hair? A few wisps. Nails and fingertips fused into one. *When will this suffering end?* they howled aloud by the time of my birth. My sisters and I carried them through the city on a palanquin with a cardboard sky and tinfoil moon. They sat perched, precious eggs, and strangers laid coins at their feet. They were as living idols, stone gods, and older still they grew. Soon I could hold them in my shirt pocket. Little breasts, they lay curled there, moaning.

IN AN OLD MAN'S HANDS

Everywhere old men are crying like babies.

Their powdered make-up cracks at the creases.

One of them tries all day to make his bed.

One of them thinks he's already dead.

One of them taps, taps, taps at the window.

One of them tries to dance with his shadow.

One of them plays an imaginary harp.

One of them licks clean the bones of a carp.

One of them stares at a doll in his lap.

One of them runs a finger along a map.

One of them wraps old letters in a flag.

One of them hears God when he coughs in a rag.

The audience shrieks and laughs in turns.

In an old man's hands, a fob watch burns.

PROMISES. FOG. GOLD. ICE.

No birds in the home, he says.

No flame in the furnace, he says.

He is a character in history.

Dirty Jew. Poor Jew. Rich Jew.

No peace in Palestine, he says.

No rest for Poland, he says.

No forgiveness for the Ukraine, he says.

No American wine, he says.

He wears a snake around his neck.

No light in the basement, he says.

No lonely window, he says.

No ocean accent, he says.

A fly rests on his open palm,

rubbing its arms against its head,

a butcher sharpening his blades.

No violin solo, he says.

No more waiting, he says.

His fingers close over the fly.

He winks his green eyes

through my daughter's face.

OO

—for Lailah

Slipping from a thousand-
year dream you came forth
and arrested me. Before
then, your beats and rests
propelled me un-toward, drops
of blood in a glass straw
taken away and tuned into
data, the night I wrung your
tempo through a twisted rag.
Shocked into light, you
hooked alien eyes to mine
and reeled, detailing the dull,
once-sterile room. Speechless,
thinner than shadow, I felt
for the first time my eyes,
heard melody made up of
silences. All the men I could
have been collapsed before
me like useless debris. You
answered my question there
and then, the question I lived.

THE SHIMMERING MAZE

Over the grand waterfall a flock
of starlings shocks me awake
at three a.m., a plate falling upward
back onto the shelf. . . .
The guests have lingered
for too long. I throw my daughter
into the air and she sticks there,
little cloud of daughter and nightgown.
The guests circle beneath her.
They agree: for her years, she's
very advanced. Gazing up,
it's difficult to imagine oneself
knee-deep in the water of *elsewhere*,
pennies hammered into coppery
satellites, humdrum days.
The bookshelf pours out words
in rain. Back to bed, my baby.
Our impurities will work themselves
out as freely as cats gather
electricity on the tips of their tongues.
I lose my place in my book.
Ink seeps up through my finger.
My pillow lays an egg.
The egg in my skull.

DEMENTIA

We are doing our rounds,
      circling the cemetery,
alphabetizing stones until
      we forget the names given us.
You kneel on the ground,
      pull tufts of grass. Startled bees
percolate around you
      in a jazzy swirl. You are
digging yourself a grave.
      Queen at the center hums
the saddest song, scats, fidgets,
      rubs her eyes, large and blind.
I put a coin on your tongue.
      I want to love you. You may
be my father, or worse yet,
      my son. Bees dip and suck,
at your grey, wispy locks,
      blind and stupid on honey.

AT THE MIDNIGHT DENTIST

He stops in mid-procedure,
touches my arm gently and asks
if everything is okay.
I give him *the big thumbs up*.
I'm sorry this is taking so long,
he says, but there's a lot unresolved here.
He clears his throat and adds, from childhood.
I feel bad for him as I have
for all my midnight dentists previously.
So much buildup, always.
And a child of Holocaust survivors
has more than his share. For instance,
I hear my father's scream
echo through the drill. Not much
I can say with a fist
in my mouth. What's that?
he asks. Nothing, nothing,
my eyes speak by squinting
and darting left and right.
Almost over, he says,
but they always say that, the midnight dentists,
even when they've just begun.
I smell the wet earth
of the Ukraine newly thawed.
I taste the dirt where what's left
of my dead grandparents lie,

the dirt my father had a cousin
fly over, in a plastic bag, from Kiev,
to one day put in his own grave
This won't hurt a bit,
says the midnight dentist, a sure sign
that it will.

BERLIN. SALT. CRICKETS.

The open grave howls at the sky.
        Let the howl be heard by all who try
to lift their neighbors out of laughter.
        Let the howl be heard by all who lathe
form out of a forest of letters,
        a sea of words. Stand back
so that the grave may breathe
        in your thoughts. Stand back
to let pass those who must pass.
        So slowly they amass at the gate.
A winter wind hews through
        a summer day. You feel it
beat against the windows. You feel it
        against your cheek. Stand back.
Let it pass through your home,
        let it creep along the floor
and caress your bare feet. Let it
        lick behind your ears, let it
wrap your heart in its palms.
        The open grave howls at the sky.
It trains its one eye at the moon
        and curses it. The morning hacks
the night to pieces. Stand back.
        Fall to the floor. Collapse.

SCALE

Today I convince myself that by doing
nothing I am getting something
done. My wife glides across the room

like a satellite. In her hands—a radiant
drink. In the next room, our daughter
sleeps, invisible waves rolling over her.

Under this water, matter so dense
you can slice it forever and still
stand there, exhausted and broken.

The radiant drink dissolves
into water that is sleep.
Our daughter sighs and, on a scale

in my mind, that little sound weighs
more than all my days filled with waves
retreating back into themselves,

leaving a negative space
that hammers against our walls.
My wife lays me down, lies down,

and stars lift off our bodies,
lock us into place, and
in a fine mist of sand, disperse.

MY DAUGHTER DRAWING

She lifts a beak to her nose and the bird
turns back to paper, its elemental form.
She knows them all now, each and every
streak of paraffin wax along the grey
sheet gutted by her tiny fingertips,
named with careful precision, the way
sentences take on the complexity of a city.
She is learning to fit into her body
and her body is learning to fit into
its landscape. I want to believe
in the cryptic nature of things,
how sense hides under layers.
But paper cannot become bird again. . .
except through her green eyes
that trace branches and leaves sprouting
miraculously from the ceiling.

FAILED EXPLANATION

I can understand why
       it's not about the money
peeling off the walls like nostalgic postcards.
          It's about precedence.
"But I'm a pornographer," she writes,
which is a pretty way of saying
      I trust your intentions,

           or *I love your scars.*
I want clarity, I think,
      or perhaps the bowl
of glistening wax fruit has nothing
to do with it.   On the other hand,
        there is always another hand.
Excuse me, but
      the pilot light in my neck
is whistling now.

WHERE WE ARE IF WE ARE NOT LOST

Your face hovers in the rusted sky,
a distant autumn letting go—
a dream of sleet and rain floats past country-slow.
Baroquely, it all falls asunder.

Draped in a fleeting breeze, I cut into silence
with silence.

                    Your wrists are thin, my love.

In water they practically disappear.

CEREMONY

The bones in the field were put there
      as a question to you. You answer, as
all answers should be, with a question.
      A hailstone knocks you on the head
and you awaken to find yourself
      balancing a pomegranate in your hand,
a fleshy felt-it-before feeling. "Father,"
      you ask, "why did you leave me here
if only to take your dinner elsewhere,
      your wine elsewhere, your quivering
cup of wine so sweet and fragrant
      it brings into sharp focus a picture of
a supplicant kneeling on a loaf of bread."
      You try on a disguise and the equation
shifts ever so slightly, throwing you to
      the ground. The bones in the field are
your bones, remember? They buried you
      here—no marker—long before my time.
The pomegranate—well, that was mine.
      How it takes in the warmth of your palms
and gives back—a pulsing, red lantern.
      The ceremony begins with a clearing
of throats and continues with a salting
      of wounds, a blindfold, a blind butterfly,
a folded note, those brittle sticks again,
      a small red ball of flesh and seeds
and a bittersweet wine so good that,
      for a second, it will make you forget all.

SYMPHONY NUMBER ONE

Why undress me,
father-confessor—
with fashionable posology?
Why praise me,
why mess with my antennae?
Why long for
the golden hypodermic,

rakish boy—
while the flames rush up
from the orchestra pit?
The pressure of needing,
likewise, leads mapmakers,
with cynical precision,
to step up the pace.

DEMENTIA

Between bedposts we float.
      We are someone else's
dream. A tractor rumbles
      by and the new moon
swells. Is it midnight or
      morning? Azalea bristle
in the breeze—first you touch
      my chest, then the house
exhales. I am thinking:
      I have seen this all before,
but I have never lived through it.

DIRGE FOR NEW AMSTERDAM

The crowds swirl odiously, cocoons that fill

our throats. A child hums, runs a finger along

the tiles. Feathers sprout on my tongue,

a useless preoccupation with flight gripping me.

Why not burrow underground? We do,

we do burrow under, we do. Why not

build a bunker to hide in? We do,

we build a secret bunker, we do, we do.

I lift you onto my back, carry you

over fields of rhododendron. We are peasants—

whose world is small, who grow spices

and smoke cheap cigarettes on the window sill.

Come, let us find somewhere quiet to

listen to the city's deep breathing,

its gasping, its emphysema.

Let's feed the ducks in the park

for the ducks are hungry, and need us, they do.

Quack, quack, they say; quack, quack, we reply.

INTOLERANCE. INDIGNITY. INDULGENCE.

I don't claim to be able to channel the gods.

I don't even claim to get the channels

on which the gods grease themselves up and challenge

one another to wrestle on plastic sheeting.

Basic cable is all I've ever had.

Not even basic. Sub-basic. Scurrilous.

For flinging mud at the window

to see the glass more clearly

is a pastime I have occasionally indulged in.

Call it a predilection. The television chirps, nudging

a disfigured starlet out of its nest.

THE SALVE

—after Donne

What can one say about days like these? Frogs have

grown wings and butterflies swim. My love, then

we have forgotten to name our new children.

We feel them paw our backs as we make love.

The television has climbed up the stairs

and settled itself at the foot of our bed;

in the heat of passion it swallows my head.

The cats at our windowsill cry out, flares

coursing over a suburban battleground,

the streets littered with squirming violins,

sleeping pills dropping like sparks to the ground.

We are tangled as wasps in raw cotton.

Try not to breathe as the smoke draws near—

these are our best days, when we shake with fear.

ASSEVERATION AFTERGLOW

If, as they say, to love is
        to sacrifice, then I ask: what
are we willing to sacrifice?
        My wife, you are disgusted
with me. We lie side by side
        in the forest. We lie

because that is what we
        do best. The sun burns
hexes through the trees,
        landing in quilt patterns on
our bed of leaves. To love is to—
        well, anything said can

be unsaid. I thought we'd
        taken our vows long ago,
sealed them under a bower of
        fruit and flowers on the upper
east side, cemented them in
        a birthing room with blips

and a constellation of blood
        across a sheet, those bright
new eyes straining to take in
        a new geometry. Yesterday,
you dreamt our daughter let in

a rat, and in the morning
I could have overlooked it
      even as it lay sprawled,
little diva of the living room,
      theatrically on its side.
When I die, asks my daughter,
      can I come back as a boy?

My doctor says I'm bleeding
      from somewhere inside.
I don't know where from,
      he says, and I'm no help—
I offer up no clues,
      only gentle waves of nausea.

There are dead leaves in my hair.
      Under my nails, dirt.
More dirt in the creases
      of my hands and feet.
No one is spared. The forest
      is burning around us.

STRAIGHT THROUGH TO MORNING

The shadow that fell between your neck and shoulders
soaked up early moonlight's butter with giddiness,
and I felt my head fill with coarse, fragrant salt,
heard the sound of clown shoes slapping the dust.
I wanted my life to gallop its way straight
through to morning, to a cooler clearing—
but it wasn't even really night yet, was it?
The words you spoke bore down like gimlets
through my spine, nearly splitting me in half,
as we made our way through the troubled forest.

THE CLOSE OF THE SILVER AGE

In the aftermath of his father's dementia

came the daughter, the rebirth. In the aftermath

of the rebirth came his wife's affair. In the aftermath

of the affair came the separation.

In the aftermath of the separation came

the reconstructed self—but he's getting ahead

of himself now, isn't he? He fears growing old,

how the embroidered wildflowers of overlapping

dendrites could entangle the whole garden.

The *garden?* He's confusing things again.

The garden has always existed "elsewhere"—

wasn't that the point of the expulsion?

Or was it the *explosion?* He throws another

volume into the fireplace. Whoosh goes

a decade in a diamond flash, in a clash

of babble, syllabic cacophony.

THE GUEST ROOM

The room you've entered is not dark at all,
another trick by your master, the bouquet

that turned out to be a garland of knives,
the diary without words, a line of inquiry

at supper: has anybody seen Saint Paul?
Anything given can as easily be taken—

Take two, and call if you should reawaken.

II

PSALM. HAMMER. WATER.

Play with me, pleads my daughter.
Her little hand fits into mine,
a plug into a socket.
She lines dolls up on the roof
of a dollhouse and knocks them
to the ground. I play the father—
little, smiling man.
I stand him up. I play again.

MICKEY MOUSE BLINKS OUT

Minnie, the pumpkin light
makes my black ears blacker,
and your polka dots are the flavor enhancers
that really get my hard-on harder.
Oh, how can you grumble about white flight
when all I want is my name in lights,
my very own neon pandemic?
Minnie, all the gladiola wine
your brown eyes brew
can't stop my love of rhetoric and fashion.
Truth is, my mouse frau, maybe we never had a chance;
I was always overcome with childish self-pity.
Aw shucks, the sirens in their hula skirts
forever jiggling along the dashboard
of my bright red Ford Roadster
sing me the *hula hula* song all day long. In all my life
I've never been so bedeviled.

MINNIE IN THE PASSENGER SEAT

Didn't I always give you our children

to eat, but alas, no good deed goes unpunished.

You licked them though they had no fur,

you licked their bald little heads.

Oh, Mickey, how could you crank

my heart round like a dachshund's tail?

Vinyl seats never made my legs as sticky

as your endearing provocations.

You're America's sweetheart, Mickey,

you're a bad boy on the lam,

a hooligan with a heart

that jumps from your shirt pocket

(oh, I remember the *thumpety-thumpety-thump* alright).

You're the one I worship, Mickey,

but still you treat me like a tourist, you rub me

the wrong way, you rob me

till I'm blind, I, who burieth *mein* claws in *thine* black ass

and screameth out: *money, money, money*.

MORTIMER MOUSE MAKES HIS CASE

You bet my car can whoop your car's ass,
and I'll razzmatazz with my suavité —
that's French for *moi!* Come with me
and I'll show you a swell swanky time.
As the good book says, "ever to do ill
is my soul's de-light." Leave that round faced
boy behind, and join claws with me.
Sure he's cute, but so are kittens. I've got
a mess of them tied up in my trunk.
Let's toss 'em in the river for fun.
Follow me, Min, and leave your litter behind.
I'll show you darkness visible, livid flames,
drugs that will make you forget your name.
I will fight *zee bull* for you, Madamouselle,
I'll make you cum using only my tail.
Just for fun we'll do it on ol' Mick's roof,
and while he's tucking all your wee ones
into bed to boot. Ain't that a hoot! My wife?
She don't care. She had an affair once
with that loony, hypochondriacal hare.
So what if we all work for the same studio?
One day it'll all be under the Stygian floodio.
Better to reign in hell than serve in heaven,
I've always said. So how about it, lil' sister?
Gimme the sign and I'll make your head spin.

DEMENTIA

Trumpeting tiger lilies stain
their legacy with lemony breath.
      Lawn mower makes the air vibrate.
A fly traversing a knee, pulsing ink blots
      beneath eyelids…
Where are the horses
 that once grazed here?

      When a cloud passes,
the manes of horses that once
grazed here meld into earth,
their hooves trample sky.
      Numbers scatter among the weeds,
a jet spikes overhead. The war is over
but it rages on. In our hearts
it rages. You hold
a hushed tiger lily.
That roars its madness into money.

THEURGY

The only thing I don't understand
is how the deaconess got her foot caught in the gravity machine

and ended up decaffeinated.
       History and physics
have an awkward way of shaking hands.

And in the end, the motel that ran midnight sports for the blind
couldn't maintain the safety valve correctly.
Thorazine encircled the city

in a kind of well-orchestrated orgy. Traumatized,
I hid under the covers. The bellboy bunny-hopped
       through the wreckage

and the Danube, more blue than bearable,
paraded past like a toy gun…

Rumors of a new kind of trout
ran rampant—but not one you'd eat:

       the kind you picture in your mind
when you can't remember the words to a prayer.

MY IRREVERENT DAYS

Now that I have reached the ripe
     age of middle-age, I will
grow two fine wings of rice
     paper and hanger wire, drape
them from my scapulae, collapsible
     beneath my raincoat. I will
use words like spice and sparks, traffic
     in promises I may not live long
enough to keep. Thus will I chart
     a new path amidst a jungle
of drunken nerve endings,
     and levitate toward my irreverent
days as effortlessly as a sunflower
     kisses a firefly's neon afterglow.

THREE APPARITIONS

1.

When the contraption
that lowered
Paul's coffin malfunctioned
everyone laughed. Paul
would have loved that,
someone said.
When he drops by
that night, I try to explain
but he waves the joke away
as one would shoo
off a tiny flying saucer,
and lights a cigarette.
These won't kill me,
he says. He says,
now that is funny.

2.

Debbie, my first suicide,
is also my first
apparition. Trouble is
she always wants to make out
and, at fifteen, I am scared stiff
with inexperience. I drool

or we drool (it's hard to tell
at fifteen). So much so
that we are soon under
water, dissolving like a couple
of pills. It's not about sex, she says.
I know, I say, feeling her slide
her tongue across
my wrist, but I can never
save her.

3.

And one night
in my fortieth year
my father comes back
to me, as if alive,
his green hospital gown
dangling open, pointing
to a map of a disintegrating
Europe, saying,
what have you done,
what have you done,
but before I can answer,
before I can open my mouth,
he sinks back into the pixilated
darkness, leaving behind a smell
of toast burning.

THE SUICIDES

The suicides always want to dance,

always want to fool around, the suicides

with their tickling fingers. their infectious laughter,

swinging their little bellies side to side against yours,

gripping the flesh along your lower back.

The suicides, with their fairy smiles,

their seductive winks, wearing the masks

of ghostly lovers, snickering into their little hands,

sneaking into gardens to steal flowers.

They love to reach under your shirt

and, when you least expect it, scratch your nipples,

run their knuckles along your collar,

blow little words into your ears,

distract you, beguile you, nuzzle

their cold noses against your ribs, leaving you

feeling betrayed, empty, a vessel

for someone else's guilt, a ship

spirited away, pirated off, at night,

and they are tormented, saddened

that you are no longer under their spell.

BEREAVEMENT IN A BLUE SKY MORNING

An elevator spirals through the eye's membrane.
                              A fuselage
high above falls away from its mother ship.

Are we destined to pray
in a bare room, in a tall white building,
          dumbfounded by those we love?

Your touch is enough to bury me
in tinsel and feathers.

WRONG NUMBER FROM ANOTHER PLANET

All of the payphones wept at once,
then promptly fell asleep. No one noticed

because this is New York. Well, one man
noticed, but no one noticed him.

I noticed him, but I was in too much of a rush
to notice myself noticing him.

That summer the subways were inexplicably
stopping between stations,

which, when under the East River,
tormented me most villainously.

I felt certain the weight of the surrounding water
combined with the vociferous flirting

of Hispanic schoolgirls in plaid skirts
was a recipe for disaster.

That was the summer when the ringing
in my head suddenly stopped.

WHAT I CALLED FOR

There's a rat scuttling beneath my ribcage looking for scraps of you.

There's a single butterfly wing fluttering in the palm of my hand.

There's a table, newly built, with your voice varnished beneath it.

There's a thorn that I kiss when I want to hear my favorite song.

There's no such thing as crime, but there are dogs trying to break the laws of gravity.

There's a date tree that grows underwater, and a kind of ballet that only sleepwalkers
    can see.

There's a scalpel so sharp it cuts between thoughts.

There's a mirror that reflects only what it wants to.

There is an ocean that tames children's hearts by holding onto their feet.

There is a hat that keeps the sky afloat above me.

There are tufts of hair that grow from the letters in this book.

There is a single word that captures everything I could ever despise.

There is someone swimming against the current, tirelessly fighting the waves, beneath
    a white cottage on a hillside,

There is a bed sheet rolling, fog atop two restless bodies.

MISCHIEF AT NIGHT

The man with the glass eye shuffles, then deals.
His shovel leans against the wall like a bored mistress.

The other men sitting at the table stare at their fingers.
A fly hunkers down on a smooth, still knuckle.

On the wooden floor a dog's tail slaps a doggy rhythm.
One man daydreams of ballerinas; another scratches his chin,

and, with his tongue, wiggles a loose tooth.
Not one of them picks up his cards before his gin.

Somewhere above their heads, a woman's laughter,
like the appearance of a sudden curve in the road.

"Ante up," titters the man with the glass eye, setting it,
with a little tap, at the center of the table. And outside?

Outside, the children tie a ribbon of firecrackers to a horse's tail.

DEMENTIA

Soon a flock of stretchers
       will dance across the heavens.
Make haste or be filled
       with lavender and lye.
Snow sticking to your cheek
       will smell of electricity.
There will be salt in your wine,
       sugar in your veins.
Trees will itch with
       spring's lost blooms.
The forgotten will be
       replaced with dead hours.
Peace be with you,
       my long lost brother,
dozing in your wheelchair
       carved from desire.

CONTRACTIONS

Are you used to the silence
oh dead one or have you come
back to strum a note or oh
to beg the cathedral one last
ballast one last new name for
oh place one hand on your breast-
bone one on your sacrum bend
your nose to knee and say the
circle say the heave ho oh say
bloody boat on the vestibule
teabag bloated in the skull
are you used to the new now
oh fallow field to the east
oh oats to the pillow heave
ho with your spine in your
hand with your hand on your
throat and oh on the bloody boat
all of it afloat oh a float

Are you start or stop or are
you stop and go oh start
where and woe or the bird
on the vestibule or is it
you with your leg on your
waist your hand on the stairs

a kind of prayer oh where

stammer and say oh where

is thine mouth my south

ballast fallen throat swollen

head to burst and a thirst

in the void which once was

rote and oh the field afresh

with (no, not) flesh and callow

and oh oh are you borne

oh oh oh can you know

the bloody boat burst ashore

and your name echoes just so

SNAPSHOT WITH ORANGE

I hold the orange,
a shrunken version
of my head, above
my head, and turn
to face the burning
glare of morning.

Mother sits,
her feet splayed apart,
a book on her lap,
its little orange heart
having blinked off
in mid-flight.

FOUND OBJECT

The kind of close that's so near
        it's more perilous than a kiss

And in it we shall carve our names
        and bless it with our fingertips

Then circle it with red crayon
        and lift it out, a coin from clay

And break it in half with a snap
        and place each *semi* on our heads

Then join together and breathe so
        close we almost touch almost

And imagine us now from above
        how strange and miraculous

We look to birds and ghosts
        our smallness bright and centered

DEMENTIA

My savior arrives
        in a wheelchair
with wings, flying
        across my retinas
as if pulled by string.

Narcotic secret
fading into a bright red eye—
the sum of each other distilled,
flowing downriver, chaste.

Another arrives,
        in a bathrobe
scraping a claw
        against the floorboards
as he sings.

THE EMPIRE OF YOUR RIGHT BREAST

I'm digging the trenches again,
hunkering down for a night
of war games, my fists stuck
in the dirt, like those of a frozen boxer.

I'm splashing in the fountain again,
wrestling with belligerent statues,
conjuring rain from a cloud of words,
jamming up the airwaves with fur.

I'm carving up the venison again,
painting strips of flesh
down the freeway, scribbling
your name across my naked chest.

I'm getting down to what most matters,
getting jiggy again with the captain
of hallelujah, ratcheting up the blankets,
making the egg cartons dance the tarantella.

I'm wiping diamonds from your lashes again,
razing the empire of your right breast,
trading deference for reverence,
conjuring up the jungle tiger's tongue.

I'm pouring an ocean into a punch bowl again,
tracing circles around a nipple
with my lips, swallowing a bellyful
of fire, praying to the black cat.

SMITTEN

I have traveled a long way

to get to where I am, after having lived

more than one life, buried an entire generation,

and now wade knee deep in cinnamon.

a bag still warm in my hands,

the diamond glare of a million stars

baring down like ecstatic pins

into my chest and neck, an iron gate, ice heavy,

before me, and behind it a garden, with peacocks

screaming into the trees,

spreading their green and black fans.

A small wooden table with

a phonograph needle

bounces along a warped dinner plate.

I am either dreaming or dead,

or more likely, I have fallen into a bliss-hole

in the soft center of our glorious fucking.

PAINTING WITH ORANGE

I peel you as I would peel an orange,
pulling back one layer
to reveal the softer, cotton-flesh
beneath, and then tender little
pouches packed with sugar
spill their juice over my fingers
and tongue as my head fills with
dreams of oranges falling from
the sky into our arms, burying us in
an hourglass of orange sand,
until time stops and we spill to the floor
like a basket of oranges, grown
hot in the sun, ready to burst.

NOWHERE

We seek out what is deep
in the core of us, digging,
victims of a famine,
using hands and mouths,
trying to reach an essential
oneness where neither of us
really exists, only a pulsing
core, the center of creation
arrived at only by burrowing
through the flesh. We have
swallowed each other and now
we are nowhere but there is
nowhere I would rather be
than nowhere in you
and you nowhere in me.

GHOSTS

A bit of you in me, a bit of me in you. When it's over and into the next day that morsel travels through the bloodstream breaking up into smaller particles swimming through the myriad channels of our bodies as if searching for a way out, an escape hatch, an eject button, but failing to find the exit, surrenders. The bits of you become part of me, the bits of me part of you. When we make love again the process repeats itself only this time the little bit of you in me has a littler bit of me in it already, the little bit of me in you has a littler bit of you already and thus over time and many nights of passionate exchange we replace each other with each other. When I knock on your door, your fist is on the other side, knocking on my door. The ghost of me smiles inside you, the ghost of you traces warm circles on the inside of my chest. When in the morning the curtain is drawn, sunlight shines through us both.

THE KINGDOM

The crystal chandelier has melted now
and at last the mattress can breathe easy.
My hands on your ass are further evidence
that we are alive, blissfully so, and something
savage is close at hand—the sound of lemons
quashed against rocks, a cartoon-giggle
from deep inside a cave? O city of your body,
high-rise of your spine, ghettos along
the hidden corners of your soft lush pubis…
If I were to travel through you
at what point would I reach the kingdom
of all I can ever be?

IMAGINARY GARDEN: AN AFTERLIFE

—for Danielle

The day is jade, but smells a little yellow,
like a pineapple, or a boy teetering on a bike,

and as church bells sound, a robin
strains to grip a centipede in its beak,

some wailing new life begins to unfurl
its makeshift wings, and I lay you down

between drops of rain, wanting nothing
but to string kisses around your collar

to cling to you like the sutures
that once dissolved into your scars.

There is a garden that only we know
how to get to—a man who sleeps

cloaked in my shadow sings there—
where all the dead I loved still waver

in a pond's reflection, where a koi breaks
the surface with its lidless eyes, and I promise

never to look away, not even to blink.

DEL SOL PRESS, based out of Washington, D.C., publishes exemplary and edgy fiction, poetry, and nonfiction (mostly contemporary, with the occasional reprint). Founded in 2002, the press sponsors two annual competitions:

THE DEL SOL PRESS POETRY PRIZE is a yearly book-length competition with a January deadline for an unpublished book of poems.

THE ROBERT OLEN BUTLER FICTION PRIZE is awarded for the best short story, published or unpublished. The deadline is in November of each year.

Full guidelines and more information are available on the website:

http://webdelsol.com